Happy Holidays!

Eid al-Fitr

by Rebecca Sabelko

BELLWETHER MEDIA
MINNEAPOLIS, MN

Blastoff! Beginners are developed by literacy experts and educators to meet the needs of early readers. These engaging informational texts support young children as they begin reading about their world. Through simple language and high frequency words paired with crisp, colorful photos, Blastoff! Beginners launch young readers into the universe of independent reading.

Blastoff! Universe

Reading Level — Grade K

Grades 1-3

Grade 4

Sight Words in This Book 🔍

a	go	many	say	to
big	here	of	see	
day	in	other	the	
each	is	our	their	
eat	it	people	they	

This edition first published in 2023 by Bellwether Media, Inc.

No part of this publication may be reproduced in whole or in part without written permission of the publisher. For information regarding permission, write to Bellwether Media, Inc., Attention: Permissions Department, 6012 Blue Circle Drive, Minnetonka, MN 55343.

Library of Congress Cataloging-in-Publication Data

LC record for Eid al-Fitr available at: https://lccn.loc.gov/2022036403

Text copyright © 2023 by Bellwether Media, Inc. BLASTOFF! BEGINNERS and associated logos are trademarks and/or registered trademarks of Bellwether Media, Inc.

Editor: Christina Leaf   Designer: Laura Sowers

Printed in the United States of America, North Mankato, MN.

Table of Contents

It Is Eid al-Fitr!

Our month
of **fasts** is over.
Eid al-Fitr is here!

A Joyful Holiday

Eid al-Fitr is a **Muslim** holiday. It follows **Ramadan**.

Eid lasts
three days.
The dates move
each year.

People end
their fast.
They honor
their beliefs.

Happy Eid!

People pray
each morning.
They go to
a **mosque**.

mosque

People visit family.
They see friends.
They say
Eid Mubarak!

They eat
a big meal.
They eat sweets.

sweets

People give to
others in need.

People give gifts.
Many give money.
Happy Eid!

Eid al-Fitr Facts

Celebrating Eid al-Fitr

family

meal

sweets

Eid al-Fitr Activities

pray

eat a
big meal

give to
others

Glossary

fasts

times when people do not eat or drink

mosque

a place where Muslims pray

Muslim

related to the Islamic faith

Ramadan

an important month-long Muslim holiday

To Learn More

ON THE WEB

FACTSURFER

Factsurfer.com gives you a safe, fun way to find more information.

1. Go to www.factsurfer.com.

2. Enter "Eid al-Fitr" into the search box and click 🔍.

3. Select your book cover to see a list of related content.

Index

The images in this book are reproduced through the courtesy of: arapix, cover (sweets), p. 23 (Ramadan); BUNDITINAY, cover (base); Aria Armoko, p. 3; kiraziku2u, pp. 4-5; nisargmediaproductions, pp. 6-7; NSFadhilatin, pp. 8-9; Pixel-Shot, pp. 10-11; ventdusud, p. 12 (mosque); sabirmallick, pp. 12-13; ibnjaafar, pp. 14-15; Veliavik, p. 16 (sweets); faidzzainal, pp. 16-17; Ferli Achirulli Kamaruddin, pp. 18-19; Willy Sebastian, pp. 20-21; Hafiza Samsuddin, p. 22 (celebrating); 4.murat, p. 22 (pray); Creativa Images, p. 22 (eat a big meal); Odua Images, p. 22 (give to others); dieddin, p. 23 (fasts); Bernhard Klar, p. 23 (mosque); dotshock, p. 23 (Muslim).